IMAGES
of America

HYDE PARK

Two young boys ride a two-seater bicycle that they have draped in canvas to resemble a sailboat during a parade in 1908. The festivities commemorated the 40th anniversary of the founding of Hyde Park.

IMAGES
of America

HYDE PARK

Anthony Mitchell Sammarco

ARCADIA

First published 1996
Copyright © Anthony Mitchell Sammarco, 1996

ISBN 0-7524-0417-2

Published by Arcadia Publishing,
an imprint of the Chalford Publishing Corporation
One Washington Center, Dover, New Hampshire 03820
Printed in Great Britain

Contents

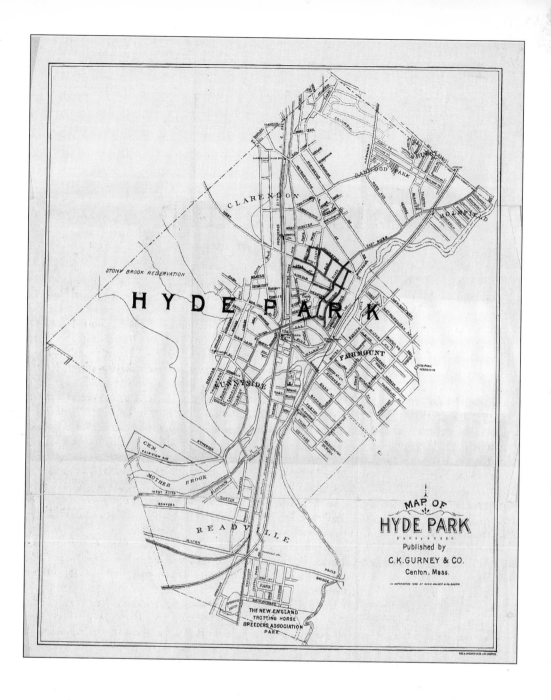

MAP OF
HYDE PARK
Published by
C.K. GURNEY & CO.
Canton, Mass.

Introduction

On January 1, 1912, Hyde Park, incorporated in 1868, ceased to exist as an independent town and became a section of Boston. It was the last of the independent Boston neighborhoods to merge officially with the larger city.

Hyde Park was created from lands ceded from Dorchester, Milton, and Dedham, Massachusetts. Located on the Neponset River with panoramic views of the Blue Hills, Hyde Park was a bucolic suburb located just 7 miles outside Boston. Henry S. Grew, who later owned the property that formed the basis for "Grew's Woods," visited the area in 1847 with his family and found the countryside's rural charms to be extraordinary. The Grews were walking in the woods and, in the words of Mr. Grew, "strolling about unexpectedly came to a point where we were very much pleased with the view of the Blue Hills and the valley in between . . . We are almost literally surrounded by woods. My friends in Boston are much surprised at my going to such a wild and lonely place."

In the next two decades, the area would be "tamed" by the Twenty Associates who built houses along Fairmount Avenue, overlooking the Neponset River. The Twenty Associates—a group of men led by Alpheus P. Blake—began the development of Hyde Park, which was named for a section of London. The men designed a prototype residence, the plans for which were used for each of the Associates' own homes. With the purchase of 100 acres at $200 per acre, the Twenty Associates laid the foundation for the town of Hyde Park.

After the election of a board of selectmen, the town grew quickly. Access to Boston by two rail lines—the Boston and Providence Railroad and the midlands branch of the New York, New Haven & Hartford Railroad—attracted new residents to the town who were equally charmed by its beauty and convenience.

From fifteen hundred residents in 1887, the town's population increased dramatically in a short period of time. Many residents of Boston's densely populated downtown area, in search of more space, "looked to the outskirts and discovered Hyde Park." With houses set on large lots of land with abundant foliage, and shopping districts, churches, and schools within walking distance, Hyde Park would become home to fifteen thousand people by the time of its annexation to Boston.

Hyde Park has a history rich in culture and tradition. In less than fifty years, the town established a legacy of pride and industry that survives to this day. Its remarkable early development as a thriving independent community is revealed in this book.

One

The Town of Hyde Park

Zenas Allen.   Benj. F. Radford.   Henry Grew.   Wm. J. Stuart.   Martin L. Whitcher.

FIRST BOARD OF SELECTMEN

The first board of selectmen of Hyde Park in 1868 were, from left to right: Zenas Allen, Benjamin F. Radford, Henry S. Grew, William J. Stuart, and Martin L. Whitcher.

Alpheus Perley Blake is considered the founder of Hyde Park and the organizer of the Twenty Associates who developed the town. The Twenty Associates, in addition to Blake, included William E. Abbott, Amos Angell, Ira L. Benton, Enoch Blake, John Newton Brown, George W. Currier, Hypolitus Fisk, John C. French, William Estabrook French, David Higgins, John S. Hobbs, Samuel Salmon Mooney, William Nightingale, J. Wentworth Payson, Dwight B. Rich, Alphonso Robinson, William H. Seavey, Daniel Warren, and John Williams.

Henry Sturgis Grew was a member of the first board of selectmen of Hyde Park and for many years was one of the commissioners of the Sinking Fund. Grew, a founder of the firm of Meredith & Grew, visited Hyde Park in 1845 and recounts that he "stopped in the woods about a half mile from where I now reside, and, strolling about, unexpectedly I came to a point where I was much pleased with the view of the Blue Hills and the valley between."

Warren Avenue in Fairmont was named for Daniel Warren (1820–1867), a member of the Massachusetts Senate as well as one of the Twenty Associates. As assistant treasurer of the Merchantile Savings Institute, Warren was a respected member of the community who also organized the Fairmount Sabbath School.

Hypolitus C. Fisk was another of the Twenty Associates. A wholesale milliner with Sleeper, Fisk, & Company in Boston, he built his house on Fairmount Avenue near Highland Street.

The Hyde Park Town Hall was a substantial Italianate building with a mansard roof. The building had served many purposes in Boston before it was moved in 1870 by wagon in sections to Hyde Park. The first floor of the town hall housed retail stores that provided income for the town. The second floor had a large room where town meetings were held from 1870 until 1911, when the residents voted to annex their town to the City of Boston.

Another view of the town hall shows a provisions store at the rear of the building. Reverend Perley B. Davis, minister of the First Congregational Church, described the town hall as "a unique structure, a remarkable combination of the grotesque, ornamental and inconvenient."

Theodore Dwight Weld (1803–1895) was the abolitionist husband of Angelina Grimke of South Carolina. As members of the anti-slavery movement, the Welds were as prominent as they were vociferous in their views. Weld was active in the community and in the establishment of the library; Weld Hall in the Hyde Park Branch, Boston Public Library, perpetuates his name.

Zenas Allen (1777–1866) was a member of the first board of selectmen of Hyde Park. Moving to Hyde Park in 1866, he was associated with the Hyde Park Woolen Company.

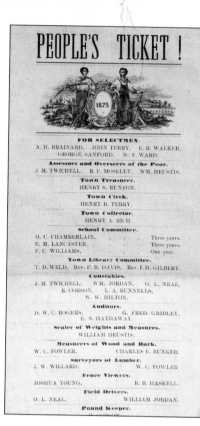

PEOPLE'S TICKET !

1875

FOR SELECTMEN.
A. H. BRAINARD,   JOHN TERRY,   E. R. WALKER,
GEORGE SANFORD,   W. F. WARD.

Assessors and Overseers of the Poor.
J. M. TWICHELL,   R. P. MOSELEY,   WM. HEUSTIS.

Town Treasurer.
HENRY S. BUNTON.

Town Clerk.
HENRY B. TERRY.

Town Collector.
HENRY A. RICH.

School Committee.
H. C. CHAMBERLAIN, ...   Three years.
E. M. LANCASTER, ...   Three years.
F. C. WILLIAMS, ...   One year.

Town Library Committee.
T. D. WELD,   REV. P. B. DAVIS,   REV. I. H. GILBERT.

Constables.
J. M. TWICHELL,   WM. JORDAN,   O. L. NEAL,
R. CORSON,   L. A. RUNNELLS,
W. W. HILTON.

Auditors.
D. W. C. ROGERS,   G. FRED. GRIDLEY,
E. S. HATHAWAY.

Sealer of Weights and Measures.
WILLIAM HEUSTIS.

Measurers of Wood and Bark.
W. C. FOWLER,   CHARLES E. BUNKER.

Surveyors of Lumber.
J. W. WILLARD,   W. C. FOWLER

Fence Viewers.
JOSHUA YOUNG,   B. B. HASKELL.

Field Drivers.
O. L. NEAL,   WILLIAM JORDAN.

Pound Keeper.

The People's Ticket for 1875 had residents running for selectmen, assessors, and overseers of the poor, as well as other positions such as fence viewers, field drivers, and pound keepers.

Henry Alexander Rich (1833–1900) was actively associated with the Real Estate and Building Company. After Hyde Park was incorporated in 1868, Rich was elected the first tax collector of the town, a "position he filled with credit for a period of ten years."

Reverend Henry Lyman built his stone house at the corner of Gordon Avenue and Austin Street. It was Lyman, a native of London, who named the town after "the beautiful and aristocratic suburb of London."

The Lyman house was later sold to Colonel John Bachelder in 1880. Bachelder was a well-known writer and the governmental historian of the Civil War's Battle of Gettysburg.

During the 40th anniversary of the founding of Hyde Park, these mounted paraders pose in front of a house with a banner that reads: "Boom The Town You Live In!"

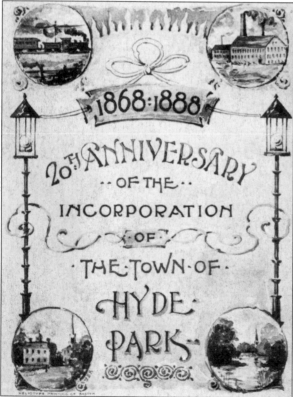

The 20th anniversary of the incorporation of Hyde Park (1868–1888) was celebrated at the town hall with a banquet followed by speeches on the accomplishments of the previous two decades.

The Hyde Park Telephone Company was the local provider of telephone service. Though Alexander Graham Bell had invented the telephone in 1877, it was not until this brick and granite building was constructed in 1904 that residents had local service. The Hyde Park Telephone Company would later be absorbed by the New England Telephone Company.

With distributing boards, transformers, and generators providing the power, these two clerks at the wire chief's desk use desk stand telephones and headphones to route calls.

Telephone operators look over their shoulders from their fifty wire switchboards in this 1911 photograph. Supervisors are pictured in the foreground, and company officials are prominent in suits and ties. For the few hundred Hyde Park residents who owned telephones, this local outlet provided smooth and efficient service.

A typical day at the Hyde Park Telephone Company had operators monitoring party lines as well as connecting incoming and outgoing telephone calls. The days of shared lines must have led to numerous complaints, but these party lines lasted in some cases until the 1950s.

A Hyde Park Boy
A Hyde Park Man

With all the Best Interests of the Town at Heart

For Representative

DR. JOSEPH M. KIGGEN

Election, Tuesday, Nov. 2, 1909

WAVERLY HALL

Dr. Joseph M. Kiggen was a candidate for representative in the election of 1909. With all the best interests of the town at heart, his campaign slogan was "A Hyde Park Boy—A Hyde Park Man."

For Representative

CLARENCE J. WING

(Formerly Town Clerk of Hyde Park)

Republican and Progressive Nominee

ELECTION, TUESDAY, NOVEMBER 5, 1912

EDWIN L. SLOCOMB, BOSTON

Clarence J. Wing was a candidate for representative in 1912. A former town clerk of Hyde Park prior to the town's annexation to Boston, Wing was the Republican and Progressive nominee for the seat.

The Hyde Park Board of Selectmen in 1891 were, from left to right: Amos H. Brainard, George L. Eldridge, Robert Bleakie, Frederick N. Tirrell, and Stephen B. Balkam.

The Hyde Park Board of Selectmen in 1905 were, from left to right: Charles E. Palmer, Howard S. Thompson, Frank B. Rich, James D. Grant, and Edwin C. Jenney.

The Hyde Park Municipal Building was built by the City of Boston after the town was annexed to Boston in 1912. This impressive Georgian Classical building is at the corner of River Street and Central Avenue.

With new streets being laid out annually, this roller smoothed the dirt roads that were ruts of mud in the spring and dust bowls in the summer. "In 1884 the selectmen began the system of grading the streets, and laying sidewalks." After Hyde Park was annexed to Boston, the roads were macadamized (finished with a compact layer of small broken stones).

A typical Hyde Park family at the turn of the century was that of Dr. Benjamin D. Weeks. The Weeks family lived at 48 Summer Street.

Jesse Wentworth Payson (1815–1889) was an author of books on penmanship in the nineteenth century. As a member of the Polytechnic Institute in Brooklyn, New York, Payson taught penmanship and bookkeeping to thousands of students. His copy books were known as the "Payson, Dunton & Scribner" series and were used as guides by many young writers.

Two
Churches

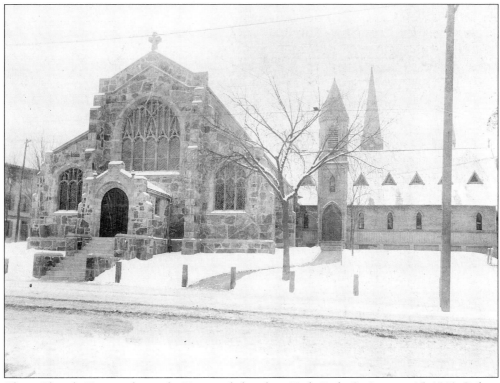

Christ Church, Episcopal, was the Episcopal church in Hyde Park. On January 15, 1893, Bishop Phillips Brooks began to raise money for the church's construction by "exhort[ing] the people to go on immediately in the work of raising funds and add[ing] to his encouraging words a gift of five hundred dollars." Opened for worship in 1894, the church was designed by Ralph Adams Cram of the architectural firm of Cram, Wentworth and Goodhue.

The First Baptist Church of Hyde Park was organized in 1858; the building was not dissimilar to other churches being built in town during the 1870s. The church boasted an impressive bell tower on the left, and a large "Welcome" sign greeted worshippers above the front doors of the church.

Reverend J.H. Gilbert was pastor of the First Baptist Church in the 1870s.

The First Congregational Church in Hyde Park was organized in 1863 and was originally on Fairmount Avenue, just east of Everett Square. In this photograph by Barritt of Hyde Park, the stick-style church with a soaring spire was set high on an embankment.

Seen from Fairmount Avenue, the First Congregational Church was adjacent to the commercial area of Everett Square.

The First Congregational Church moved to the corner of Webster Street and Central Avenue. The new church was designed by the firm of Kilham & Hopkins and was built in 1911. It was an impressive example of the American Gothic-style in Weymouth seam-face granite.

Reverend A.H. Washburn took charge of Christ Church in Hyde Park in 1861 and was elected rector in January 1862. It was while he served at this parish that the first church structure was built.

The Episcopal church in Hyde Park was organized in 1860 with Reverend A.H. Washburn as its first pastor. The first church was consecrated on December 1, 1863, and is shown here in 1872. A granite and rail fence borders the property at the corner of River and Maple Streets.

Children of the Sunday school of Christ Church, Episcopal, celebrate Washington's Birthday in 1892. In uniforms, periwigs, and hats that recreate those worn in the era of General Washington, these boys and fair maidens of the Sunday school pose outside the church, all the while being watched by their friends from the windows.

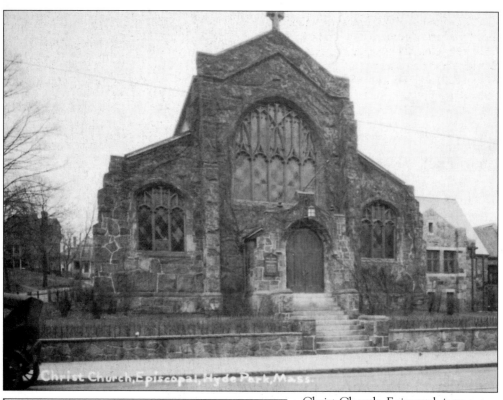

Christ Church, Episcopal, Hyde Park, Mass.

Christ Church, Episcopal, is an impressive stone church at the corner of River and Maple Streets. Designed by the noted architect Ralph Adams Cram, the church is now listed on the National Register of Historic Places.

DEDICATION

OF THE

Hazelwood Universalist Church

OF

HYDE PARK, MASS.

Sunday, October 1, 1893,

AT 3 P.M.

The Hazelwood Universalist Church was dedicated on October 1, 1893.

Reverend Francis C. Williams was called to the Hyde Park Unitarian Church in 1870, three years after it was organized. Reverend Williams was also secretary of the Hyde Park School Committee in the 1870s.

The interior of the Unitarian church in Hyde Park had a banner that read: "I Am The Resurrection And The Life." The first meeting of the church was held in 1867, after which the members incorporated themselves as "The Christian Fraternity." The church was dedicated on February 18, 1875, with Reverend Williams as pastor.

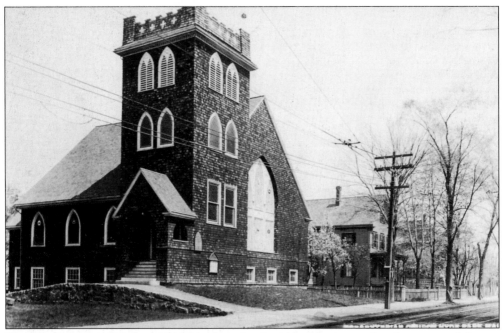

The Presbyterian church was a shingle-style church with a crenelated tower and lancet windows. The Presbyterian Church is a traditional Calvinistic denomination governed by presbyters, or elders.

The Methodist Episcopal church was organized in 1867 and was a stick-style, wood-framed building. Members of this Protestant Christian church adhere to the teachings of John Wesley.

Most Precious Blood Church is at the corner of Maple and Oak Streets. Created as a separate parish in 1870, a small wood-framed church was built in 1875 to serve the Catholics of Hyde Park. The cornerstone of the present church was laid on July 4, 1880.

The nave of Most Precious Blood has an impressive arched ceiling that leads to a marble altar.

Saint Anne's Church was dedicated on October 23, 1921, with Father David Regan serving as its first pastor. Serving the Catholics of Readville for over sixty years, Saint Anne's was substantially rebuilt and dedicated by Humberto Cardinal Medeiros on May 30, 1982.

Saint Joseph's Church, built in 1956, was dedicated by Richard Cardinal Cushing. Created a separate parish in 1938, Saint Joseph's originally met in the Sullivan Mill on Hyde Park Avenue. The new church was built at the corner of Wood and Irwin Avenues (now Chapel Road).

Saint Pius Tenth Church is on Wolcott Street in Milton on the Hyde Park line.

In this 1910 photograph, Most Precious Blood dominates the corner of Maple and Oak Streets with its soaring spire. The church is 137 feet long and 68 feet wide; the spire is 162 feet high.

The Clarendon Congregational Church was organized in 1880 and was remodeled in 1911. In a "shingle certificate," it was said that by purchasing this card the "main entrance is to be nearly level with the sidewalk, and broad stairways will lead to the audience room and to the vestry."

The Clarendon Congregational Church was at the corner of Collins Street and Huntington Avenue. The simple, wood-framed church was unfortunately destroyed by fire.

Three
Schools

The Butler School was established in 1804 by the Town of Dorchester for students in the western section of that town, which became Hyde Park in 1868. The school was named in 1850 after Reverend Henry Butler, "a teacher in the public schools of the town [of Dorchester] more than two hundred years ago."

The Greenwood School was an elementary school in Hyde Park. The school was named for Elihu Greenwood, a member of the Dorchester School Committee before the town was annexed to Boston in 1870. Students pose here in 1878 on the school lawn.

The second grade of the Greenwood School posed outside for this class photograph in 1906. A new Greenwood School was built on Metropolitan Avenue in 1957, and was designed by John M. Gray.

The Grew School was built in 1871 in the Sunnyside area of Hyde Park, and was named for Henry Sturgis Grew. A new Grew School was built on Gordon Avenue in 1958, designed by J. Guarino.

The students of Eudora Harlow Brigham, a fourth-grade teacher at the Grew School, posed for a class picture on May 16, 1899. The banner with the oval portrait of George Washington surmounted by an eagle was used by a photographer who went from school to school taking class photographs.

The members of the Grew School Orchestra pose for a photograph in 1902. With drums, bass viols, violins, flutes, and horns, the orchestra would perform for their fellow students and give evening recitals for their parents, teachers, and friends.

Baseball players of the Hyde Park High School pose in 1908.

The Fairmount School served students in the Fairmount section of Hyde Park. Built in 1871, it was initially known as the Blake School in honor of Alpheus P. Blake. It was renamed in 1875 after "agitation by some citizens to preserve the old name of Fairmount in connection with the school finally prevailed."

Fourth-grade students of the Fairmount School pose in 1899 in front of the traveling banner of Washington.

The new Fairmount School was built in 1953 on Williams Avenue. Designed by T.F. McDonough, it was a modern school for its time.

Even young boys learned practical arts at the Fairmount School. Here, a student tries his hand at a sewing machine.

The Hyde Park High School, photographed in 1875, was an Italianate school with separate entrances for boys and girls. The school had four rooms and, though an annex was added in 1889, it proved insufficient for the number of students in attendance. The first diplomas were awarded in 1873.

Members of the Hyde Park High School Battalion pose in the rear of the school while some of their fellow students watch from windows.

Merle S. Getchell was principal of the Hyde Park
High School at the turn of the century.

Students in the Hyde Park High School Class of 1890 pose in front of the school for their
class picture.

Miss Mary Alson Knight was one of the "belles" of the Hyde Park High School Class of 1892. During the graduation exercises at Waverly Hall, Knight read "The Battle with the Pirates" from *Ben-Hur*.

Frederic Herbert Bass was a member of the battalion of the Hyde Park High School in 1892.

Fred M. French was a member of the Class of 1900 at Hyde Park High School. As a member of the Boys' Battalion, he wore a distinctive uniform with brass buttons and a gold braid on his cap.

Members of the Hyde Park High School Band pose on the school grounds with George E.M. Dickinson, their conductor.

In 1905, the football team of the Hyde Park High School won 12–0 in a game against Dorchester High School.

Members of the basketball team of Hyde Park High School pose in 1909 with their coach, who is on the far right in the back row.

Hyde Park High School was built at the corner of Harvard and Everett Streets. An impressive school of brick and limestone, it was designed by the Boston architectural firm of Loring & Phipps. Completed in 1902, this building was used until a new high school was built. The original Hyde Park High School then became the William Barton Rogers School, named for the founder and first president of the Massachusetts Institute of Technology.

The girls' basketball team of Hyde Park High School poses in the gymnasium in 1952.

The third, and present, home of Hyde Park High School was completed in 1928 and is at the junction of Metropolitan and Central Avenues. With an impressive pedimented entry and urn finials above, the new high school is one of the most elegant schools in Boston.

Students of the Hyde Park High School wave to the photographer in November 1945.

The Hyde Park High School Cadets pose at Kelley Field, opposite the cotton mill on River Street. The officers in 1949 were, from left to right: Robert Case (in back), ? Di Petro, Francis Curran (in back), Chester Molinari, Elmer Langley, and Ronald Dacko. Dr. Francis J. Horgan, headmaster of Hyde Park High School, is in a suit standing between the cadets.

Shop class was a perquisite for boys in the Boston school system whether they were in the college course or not. Here the shop teacher, on the left, shows his remarkably well-dressed shop students how to use a drill. Looks exciting!

Four
Clubs and the Library

A "George Washington Reception" was held in Hyde Park in 1871. Present at the reception were, from left to right: Miss Mary Leseur, Dr. R.R. Andrews, Reverend George Pike, Miss Georgie Clark, David Angell, Miss Jennie Hammond, Daniel J. Goss (in rear with beard), R.W. Turner, Miss Mary Washburn (in rear), Miss Addie Gilpatrick, George Angell, Miss Lizzie Leseur, and Timothy Foster.

The Hyde Park Clubhouse was a fanciful Italianate house with a piazza extending along the front and side. With parlors, a dining room, and a billiard room, members of the club could relax in comfort while enjoying the company of their fellow members.

George M. Rice was president of the Hyde Park Club at the turn of the century. Organized in 1889, the club's officers included G. Fred Gridley (vice president), George E. Whiting (treasurer), and Charles F. Light (secretary).

The Peabody Home for Crippled Children provided care for the physically disabled.

The Hyde Park Horticultural Society was founded in 1884 with William Ellery Channing serving as the first president. In September 1891, members of the society exhibited their fruits, vegetables, and flowers at the Hyde Park Town Hall, in hopes of winning awards.

The Hyde Park & Fairmount Literary Association hosted a lecture by Wendell Phillips on December 31, 1866, at the Music Hall. Phillips' speech was entitled "The Lost Arts." These lyceum lectures, as well as programs of live music held at the Association, greatly appealed to residents in the days before radio and television.

The Hyde Park Library was completed in 1899 at the corner of Harvard Avenue and Winthrop Street. A Grecian Ionic building, its "foundation is of hammered Deer Isle granite and the walls are of gray Roman brick, with terra cotta trimmings. The inside finish is of oak, with the exception of that in the main reading room."

The library became the Hyde Park Branch, Boston Public Library, when the town was annexed to Boston on January 1, 1912. On the left is the old Hyde Park High School, now the William Barton Rogers School.

Looking down Harvard Avenue toward Winthrop Street in 1910, the library was near the central firehouse at the corner of Winthrop Street and Harvard Avenue.

"We shake tonight Gentlemen,
But not with fear."

Gentlemen's Night
Hyde Park Current Events Club
Wednesday Evening, February 14th, 1906
WAVERLY HALL

Eight to Twelve O'clock

COMMITTEE IN CHARGE
Mrs. G. W. Pfeiffer

Mrs. J. E. Horr	Mrs. I. C. Porter
Mrs. J. E. Cotter	Mrs. W. N. Beal
Mrs. S. A. Tuttle	Mrs. C. A. Easton

The Hyde Park Current Events Club was a prominent women's club in town. On February 14, 1906, the club hosted "Gentlemen's Night" at Waverly Hall. On that occasion, club members said, "We shake tonight Gentlemen, But not with fear." It sounds like a lively dance was enjoyed!

The Odd Fellows Block in Everett Square housed businesses on the first floor with a hall above. The Odd Fellows organization originated during the Industrial Revolution to secure a system of benefits to assist members during hard times. The first American lodge of Odd Fellows was in Baltimore in 1819; affiliated local groups were quickly formed throughout the United States.

The Hyde Park Association of the Young Mens Christian Association (YMCA) was organized in 1885. With ninety-five active and thirty-five associate members, organizers heard "a loud call from our young men for a gymnasium, which we earnestly desire to add as soon as our finances allow." The generous donation of Edward Ingersoll Brown financed the construction of a gymnasium on River Street, designed by New York architect Thomas Rowe.

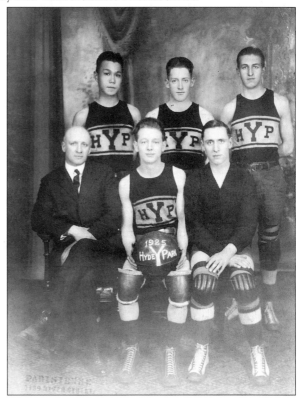

Members of the basketball team of the Hyde Park "Y" pose in 1925. From left to right are: (front row) Mr. Dana Sears, unknown, and unknown; (back row) George Onishi, Roy Boyd, and Bob Bruce.

The Hyde Park YMCA is a noble structure. When he donated the funds for its construction, Mr. Brown stated that the building "should be in all respects in good taste." Said Brown: "Make the first story of granite and the second of the best faced brick. Let the principal story be finished in hardwood." This building, whose association benefits the young men of Hyde Park physically, mentally, morally, and spiritually, still carries forth the wishes of Edward Ingersoll Brown.

The Hyde Park YMCA basketball team members in 1931 were, from left to right: (front row) Freddie Giesel, Albert Briggs, Bob Bruce, Roy Boyd, George Onishi, and Mr. Dana Sears, (coach); (back row) Ralph Bates, Joseph Boyd, Sam Smyth, Johnny "Bull" Mahen, Arthur Macklis, and Carl Bartho.

Five

Everett Square and Cleary Square

Everett Square is the junction of River and Way Streets and Fairmount and Central Avenues. The Fairmount Block (on the right) was built in 1872 by Charles Cobb; the Bank Building (center) was built in 1875 by A.H. Holway. Everett Hall, on the third floor of the Bank Building, was dedicated on December 30, 1875, with a grand concert.

Everett Square, photographed in 1876, shows children around the flagpole in the center of River Street. The house on the left was built in 1873 by Dr. Willard S. Everett.

Fairmount Avenue, looking toward Everett Square, was photographed in 1876 with the Stevens Building, built in 1868, on the right. The long brick building in the center was the Beates Block, built in 1872 by John Beates, and the next structure was built by Leonard Alder in 1871. The furthest building was the Odd Fellows Hall.

A group of young ladies ride past Liberty Hall in Everett Square in the late 1860s. On the first floor was C.H. Abbott's Groceries and Provisions Store.

In 1876, River Street was photographed looking toward the Hyde Park station of the New York, New Haven & Hartford Railroad.

The Everett house was a noted hotel located at the corner of River and Maple Streets. Opened in 1868 by Alpheus P. Blake and J.C. Carr, it was operated by O.C. Coffin, the well-known manager of the American House in Concord, New Hampshire. Named for Edward Everett, onetime governor of Massachusetts and a prominent statesman, the building was kept as a hotel until 1877.

The grocery store of George Miles was on River Street. Mr. Miles carried "one of the largest and best assorted stocks of groceries in the town, including everything from the staple and fancy line and provisions, except meats." According to the same report, "He ma[de] a specialty of high-grade teas and coffees and fine creamery butter from St. Albans, Vermont."

Haskell's Shoe Store was in the Masonic Block. Shown here in 1902, the store is cluttered with shoe boxes. Haskell's also sold canes and umbrellas to augment their shoe sales.

Henry Routley was photographed in front of his custom tailor shop in the 1880s. His shop was opposite the Masonic Temple, and he offered the cleaning and pressing of pants at 75¢.

The Neponset Block was on Fairmount Avenue, next to the First Congregational Church. The church spire can be seen on the left.

The Hyde Park Caramel Company was on River Street. There, G.H. Roberts "manufacture[d] all kinds of caramels, chocolates, bonbons and counter candies." So popular were his caramels that they "had a reputation in Boston and elsewhere for their excellence." Ice cream was served on the right, and confections could be purchased on the left.

The Everett Square Theatre was built on the site of the Neponset Block. The theatre's offerings included not only movies, but vaudeville acts as well in the early 1920s. The theatre later became the Pixie and, most recently, the Riverside Theatre Works.

Felix Henry was a well-known vaudeville actor who often performed at the Everett Square Theatre.

Oak Street runs from Hyde Park Avenue to Pine Street near Everett Square. The houses built in the mid-nineteenth century created a pleasant neighborhood with picket fences, trees, and lush green lawns.

Another view of Oak Street shows the mature oak trees that were planted when the street was laid out.

Looking down River Street from Everett Square toward Cleary Square, one observes tracks in the center of the street for streetcars. On the right is Maple Street (the lawn of Christ Church is visible), and on the right is Harvard Avenue.

Cleary Square is the junction of River Street and Hyde Park Avenue. The intersection was named in 1899 in memory of John A. Cleary, a soldier of Company G, 7th Regiment, who lost his life in Santiago during the Spanish-American War. The son of John Cleary of 617 Hyde Park Avenue, this local hero was "the first of the many brave young men who enlisted from Hyde Park to fall in defense of his country."

Cleary Square, looking from Hyde Park Avenue toward River Street, features Kennedy's Block on the left. Kennedy's Clothing and Shoe Store was known as "Hyde Park's greatest mercantile establishment"; the store was founded in 1894 and later moved to Summer Street in downtown Boston. The other tenants of the Kennedy Block in 1908 were Burnes Brothers, The Mammoth, Robert Karnan Dry Goods Store, J.E. Farrell Hardware and Paint, and Taylor's Bowling Alleys.

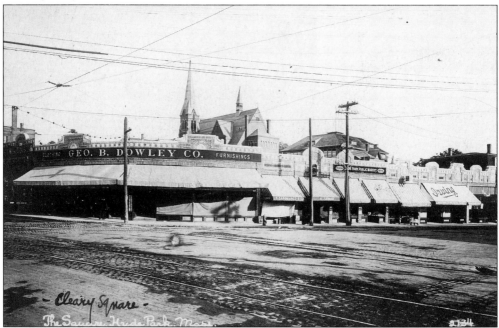

The George B. Dowley Company, a well-known company providing clothing and furnishings, was at the corner of Hyde Park Avenue and River Streets. The spire of Most Precious Blood Church rises above the store. The corner is now occupied by Papa Gino's.

The Hyde Park station of the New York, New Haven & Hartford Railroad was on River Street, opposite the Kennedy Block. A stucco station with a Spanish tile roof, it was an impressive addition to Cleary Square. The iron railing on the left still survives on River Street.

The Hyde Park railroad station was at street level. Passengers descended by a covered staircase to the platform to await their train.

Cleary Square was a thriving commercial district in 1908, the year this postcard was produced. The railroad provided service to Boston, as did streetcars along Hyde Park Avenue and River Street.

In the 1950s, Cleary Square was a major shopping area for not just for residents of Hyde Park but also for people from Dedham, Milton, and Dorchester. Looking down River Street toward Everett Square, classic automobiles give the square a different feeling than that at the turn of the century.

Six
Fairmount

This view of Fairmount from Mount Neponset in 1857 was first published in *Ballou's Pictoral Drawing-Room Companion*. A train from the New York, New Haven & Hartford Railroad passes in the foreground, and sailboats glide along the Neponset River. The new houses of the Twenty Associates can be seen along Fairmount Avenue. The central house across the bridge was the first house built by the Twenty Associates in 1856 for George W. Currier.

In 1858 there was a public sale of "many of the most desirable Building Sites at Hyde Park & Fairmount." A special train was chartered from the Boston and Providence depot at Park Square in Boston for buyers to attend the sale of these suburban lots.

The Fairmount Avenue Bridge was photographed in 1876 from the Neponset River looking up Fairmount toward Milton.

The Fairmount Station was on the midland branch of the New York, New Haven & Hartford Railroad; also on this line were the River Street and Glenwood Avenue stops. Here a man waits on the platform for his train, which connected Hyde Park to Boston in fifteen minutes.

The Fairmount Avenue station crossing ran parallel with the Neponset River. Though most engines belched smoke and make a fierce racket, these railroad crossings were hazardous for pedestrians and people were warned to "Look out for the engine."

Looking toward Fairmount from the banks of the Neponset River in 1888, it is easy to see why Hyde Park was attractive to visitors. The lush lawns, majestic trees, and panoramic vistas combined to form a suburban haven that was also convenient to Boston.

Water Street was photographed in the winter of 1895 from Fairmount Avenue looking toward Dana Avenue. The street would not be plowed but "rolled": a heavy roller was pulled by horses to pack the snow for sleighs.

Looking toward the Neponset River from the top of Fairmount Avenue in 1872 provided a dramatic panorama of Hyde Park.

Fairmount Avenue was the site of one of the houses built by the Twenty Associates.

The Alpheus J. Robinson house was at the corner of Water Street and Fairmount Avenue. A man in a rowboat pulls in front of the house in the 1860s.

The Robinson house, looking from Fairmount Avenue, was a substantial residence with a barn in the rear. Robinson was a member of the Twenty Associates and enjoyed the title of "professor." He was proficient in music and was president and leader of the Hyde Park and Fairmount Choral Society.

The house of Alpheus Perley Blake was located at 24 Norway Park. A turreted villa set on extensive grounds, it was occupied by Blake's descendants until the 1950s.

Jesse W. Payson's house at 272 Fairmount Avenue (built in 1856) was a winter wonderland in this 1889 photograph. Payson was a member of the Twenty Associates.

Shown here in 1915, 71 Greenwood Avenue was not on Fairmount but was located between Metropolitan and Hyde Park Avenues. It was a typical Italianate house, similar to those built by the Twenty Associates on Fairmount.

The Frederick N. Tirrell house was built at the corner of Beacon and Pleasant Streets, overlooking the Neponset River. Built with a substantial stone foundation and stone piers marking the edges of the property, this Queen Anne house was among the grandest of the late-nineteenth-century houses built in Fairmount.

John C. Hunter's house was at 21 Water Street. Built by William Roberts, moderator of the first town meeting in Hyde Park, the house was updated in the 1880s with stick-style detailing.

William H. Seavey built his house at 192 Fairmount Avenue in 1856. Later purchased by Benjamin F. Radford, who made extensive changes to the house and property, the house was photographed in 1899.

William J. Stuart's house was at 55 Water Street. Stuart served as representative to the general court in 1879.

Water Street was leveled in the 1950s to make way for Truman Highway, a modern thoroughfare connecting Mattapan Square to the Neponset Valley Parkway named for President Harry S. Truman. After the construction of Truman Highway, Water Street ceased to exist except in a short area opposite Faraday Street. Here, cranes finish the leveling of the area in advance of the road construction.

Seven
Central Avenue and Clarendon Hills

Central Avenue runs from River Street at Everett Square to Westminster Street. Between the Civil War and the turn of the century, many substantial houses were built along this tree-lined street.

This view is looking down Central Avenue from River Street in the 1880s. On the right is the store built in 1869 by Dwight B. Rich, a member of the Twenty Associates. The Methodist church, on the left, was built in 1874. The Odd Fellows Building, on the immediate left, was built in 1864 by William H. Ingersoll, a merchant tailor.

Known as Rich's Block by the turn of the century, this building housed stores on the first floor and the photographic studio of Warren of Hyde Park on the second and third floors (the Warren studio is responsible for this photograph). On the first floor, on the left, was the first location of the Hyde Park Library.

Gordon Avenue was photographed in 1876 with the town hall (on the left) and the Willard House, a hotel opened in 1873 by James W. Willard. Mr. Charles Crummall and his son are on the right side of the group of people in the center of the street.

Photographed in 1906, the Scott house was at the corner of Harvard Avenue and Winthrop Street. The house was purchased by Thomas McDonough "for $80.00, and [was] removed to Central Avenue, near Arlington Street and converted to tenements." That year, the new fire station was built on the site shown here.

These two houses are at the corner of Warren Avenue and Highland Street. The Angell house (on the left) was built in 1861 by the sons of Moses Angell; the house on the right was built in 1878 by Edwin C. Aldrich.

T. Emery Clark built this house at 78 Pierce Street in 1870, and sold it in 1889 to John McDougald. McDougald, a foreman of the S.B. Balkam & Company, was also captain of Chemical Engine No. 1 in Hyde Park.

John N. Pickett built his house in 1878 at 20 Neponset Avenue. Pickett was both a carpenter and a builder; his house was typical of those being built in this period.

Stephen Brewer Balkam built his house at 113 Central Avenue. A lumber and coal dealer under the corporate name of S.B. Balkam & Company, Balkam provided much of the lumber necessary for the new houses being built in Hyde Park after he moved to town in 1874.

Charles Vose built his house at 57 Milton Avenue in 1871. A description of the house when it was for sale in 1890 said that it had "11 rooms, including bathroom; in excellent repair, including chandeliers, curtains, storm doors and windows, good furnace, hot and cold water, and a large and handsome piazza."

The corner of Oak and Maple Street had large houses with ample lawns and curving streets. Though not on Central Avenue, the houses were set high on the hill and overlooked the houses toward Clarendon Hills and the Blue Hills.

Central Avenue had a wide variety of housing styles by the turn of the century, including Italianate, Queen Anne, stick-style, and Colonial Revival.

This house at 116 Central Avenue (c. 1888) was given an extravagant Queen Anne piazza along the facade at the turn of the century. Piazzas— literally, covered porches—always had sky blue ceilings to replicate the sky.

The Square at Clarendon Hills was dedicated with great pomp in the first decade of the twentieth century. Clarendon Hills is the area of Hyde Park Avenue near the Roslindale line.

Henry A. Rich built this block at Clarendon Hills Square in the 1880s.

Henry L. Willard built his house at 256 Hyde Park Avenue, at the corner of Arlington Street.

Hazelwood was one of three stations in Hyde Park on the Boston and Providence Railroad; Hyde Park Center and Readville were the other two. On the right is the taxidermist shop of Frank Blake Webster. His "Museum & Naturalists' Supply Depot" boasted a museum and curiosity shop of "animals, birds eggs, land and marine curios" that were preserved, mounted, and displayed for the public's inspection.

The Bulloch house in Readville was a typical mid-eighteenth-century farmhouse. Originally built by the Damon family, the house stood on Readville Street between Damon Street and Damon Place.

The Badlam house was the "oldest house in town" when it was photographed in 1889. The Badlams had settled in Dorchester in the early seventeenth century and were a noted family of cabinetmakers in the Dorchester Lower Mills.

Eight

Readville

The Neponset River passes through Readville at the Dedham line. The marshes and the three arches of Paul's Bridge make for a scenic view at the turn of the century. Originally known as the "Dedham Low Plain," Readville was renamed in 1847 for James Read, of Read & Chadwick, principal owner of the cotton mill in this part of Hyde Park.

Paul's Bridge connects Hyde Park and Milton. Rebuilt in stone in the mid-nineteenth century, the bridge was a major connector that still is used. Wood railings span the bridge, protecting walkers and carriages from falling into the Neponset River.

Ebenezer Paul was a member of the family for whom Paul's Bridge was named. The Paul Farm had been laid out by his ancestor in 1719 and the family homestead was at the corner of River Street and Glenwood Avenue.

The Readville railroad station was a passenger depot on the Providence division of the New York, New Haven & Hartford Railroad.

These workmen are finishing the bridge at Hyde Park Avenue in 1899.

A horse-drawn wagon ascends the incline at the grading for Hyde Park Avenue in Readville. The grading was between the Readville station of the Providence division of the New York, New Haven & Hartford Railroad and the old station of the New England Railroad.

The Sprague Street bridge, between Milton and Horne Streets, is shown here under construction in 1899.

Walcott Square, the junction of Prescott Street, Neponset Valley Parkway, and Walcott Court, was named in honor of Governor Roger Wolcott. Wolcott served as governor of Massachusetts between 1896 and 1898.

This photographer poses beside his tripod camera under a road sign that says "Hyde Park 1 1/2 miles." These road signs, though small, directed the new "horseless carriages" through the maze of city streets.

The Readville Trotting Park was a popular racetrack; a special spur of the railroad brought spectators from Boston to watch the races daily. The trotting park was located partially on the grounds of Camp Meigs, a training ground for Union soldiers during the Civil War. The camp, which was named after Montgomery Meigs, was undeveloped until the 1890s when "one of the finest race tracks in the world" was laid out.

George N. races at the Readville Trotting Park in 1907. Driven by Fred C. Garmon, George N. had a trial of 2:07 1–4.

Uhlan (on the left) is seen defeating Hamburg Belle at the Readville Trotting Park in 1909.
Robert C. Proctor (in the inset portrait) drove Uhlan to victory and received a silver loving
cup.

Miss Pratt (on the left) is in a head-to-head race at the homestretch with Billie Taylor. Miss
Pratt, driven by Benjamin Pope, won the race at 2:17 1–4.

These Readville friends and World War II veterans are, from left to right: Albert Pascuito, Richard Nedder, Alice Imbaro, and George Nedder. They were photographed in 1945 on Blanchard Road in Readville; the street was renamed Imbaro Road in 1950 in memory of Frank Imbaro, whose death in 1949 was a result of his service in World War II. Lucy Imbaro, a Gold Star Mother, had four children who served in World War II: Alice, Frank, Nicholas, and Guido.

Nine

Police and Fire Departments

Members of the Hyde Park police force pose on the steps of the Hyde Park Library in 1910. From left to right are: (in front) Captain Robert Grant and Lieutenant Edward Welch; (first row) Alexander Herring, Frank Whitticker, Edward Sheppard, W. Runnels, George Tucker, and O. McMahon; (back row) William Downey, Andrew Cullen, Eldridge Dyer, Thomas Meighan, and Rodger Flaherty.

The pumper "Hancock" served the needs of the Hyde Park Fire Department for nearly half a century. The tub of the horse-drawn engine would be filled with water from buckets; firemen would then "pump" the levers of the engine to create a powerful stream of water that could be pointed at the fire and, hopefully, extinguish it.

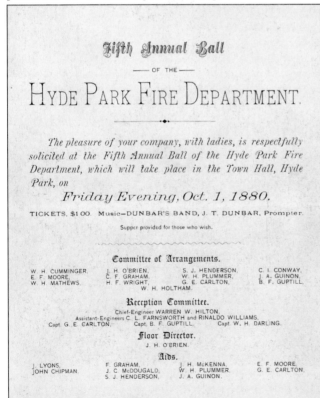

𝔉𝔦𝔣𝔱𝔥 𝔄𝔫𝔫𝔲𝔞𝔩 𝔅𝔞𝔩𝔩

— OF THE —

HYDE PARK FIRE DEPARTMENT.

The pleasure of your company, with ladies, is respectfully solicited at the Fifth Annual Ball of the Hyde Park Fire Department, which will take place in the Town Hall, Hyde Park, on

Friday Evening, Oct. 1, 1880.

TICKETS, $1.00. Music—DUNBAR'S BAND, J. T. DUNBAR, Prompter.

Supper provided for those who wish.

Committee of Arrangements.

W. H. CUMMINGER,	J. H. O'BRIEN,	S. J. HENDERSON,	C. I. CONWAY,
E. F. MOORE,	C. F. GRAHAM,	W. H. PLUMMER,	J. A. GUINON,
W. H. MATHEWS,	H. F. WRIGHT,	G. E. CARLTON,	B. F. GUPTILL,
		W. H. HOLTHAM.	

Reception Committee.

Chief-Engineer WARREN W. HILTON,
Assistant-Engineers C. L. FARNSWORTH and RINALDO WILLIAMS,
Capt. G. E. CARLTON,   Capt. B. F. GUPTILL,   Capt. W. H. DARLING.

Floor Director.

J. H. O'BRIEN.

Aids.

J. LYONS,	F. GRAHAM,	J. H. McKENNA,	E. F. MOORE,
JOHN CHIPMAN.	J. C. McDOUGALD,	W. H. PLUMMER,	G. E. CARLTON.
	S. J. HENDERSON,	J. A. GUINON.	

The 5th annual ball of the Hyde Park Fire Department was held at the town hall on October 1, 1880. Supper was followed by a dance of quadrilles, marches, and waltzes to the music of Dunbar's Band. Ladies' dance cards had spaces where their dancing partners for the evening would write their names. All dancing was under the direction of J.H. O'Brien, floor director.

The old "Hancock" was photographed at the turn of the century. From the metal rods above the engine were hung leather buckets that were used to convey water to fill the engine tub. With horses racing wildly to the scene of the fire, a conflagration a century ago must have created great excitement.

The Central Fire Station was a two-story wood building that housed the new chemical engines of the fire department. The belfry had a bell that was tolled to alert the firemen to meet at the firehouse and "suit up" before going to fight the fire.

Members of the Hyde Park Fire Department pose in 1905 outside the Central Fire Station. From left to right are: (front row) John McDougald, Chief John Wetherbee, and Frank Kunkel; (back row) Edward Bullard, William McDougald, Michael Foley, Dennis Mahoney, and Frank Mercer.

The horse-drawn fire engines pose outside the firehouse on Hyde Park Avenue at the turn of the century. The firemen, from left to right, are: ? Wandlass, ? Whittemore, Fred Hawley, and Edward Hawley.

The new Central Fire Station was built on Central Avenue at the corner of Harvard Avenue in the Romanesque revival style.

The interior of the Central Fire Station, in 1972, had a modern fire engine that had extension ladders, hoses, and fire-fighting equipment, a far cry from the original "Hancock" of a century before.

Hyde Park firemen pose with their Amoskeag fire engine in Grew's Woods in 1890. On the left one of the firemen holds a silver trumpet, used not just as a ceremonial badge of office but also for shouting orders during a fire.

No matter how modern or well-trained a fire department, some fires can still prove disastrous. This duplex building was at the corner of Hyde Park Avenue and River Street, opposite Kennedy's Clothing Store, and was destroyed by a fire in the winter of 1882.

Ten

Industries

This horse-drawn delivery wagon was the typical means of transportation a century ago.

The Hyde Park Company was founded in 1882 by Joseph S. Hamblin. Summering in Hyde Park in 1861 and "charmed by its healthful attractions," Hamblin built a house on Williams Avenue and later opened this fine art gravures—or print—factory in town.

The Fairmount Manufacturing Company was founded in 1874 by Charles A. House. The company manufactured ladies' shirtwaists and muslin underwear.

The American Tool & Machine Company manufactured not only sugar machinery but also tools, hangers, shafting, and pulleys. Founded in 1848 and organized in 1864, the factory employed over three hundred workers; most of the machinery it produced was used in the sugar refineries of the Sandwich Islands, Cuba, and the West Indies.

Benjamin Franklin Radford was president and general manager of the American Tool & Machine Company.

The machinery produced by the American Tool & Machine Company included: turret and brass lathes, belt knife-leather-splitting machines, belt knives, shafting, hangers, pulleys, centrifugal sugar machines and extractors, wood pulp digesters, millwright work, and general machinery.

These workmen outside the American Tool & Machine Company were among the three hundred factory workers employed by the company at the turn of the century.

Scott's Scouring Mill was founded in 1874 in the Milton Lower Falls, but relocated to Hyde Park eight years later. Two million pounds of wool was "scoured" annually at the mill for the large number of wool manufacturers in Boston.

John Scott was the founder of Scott's Scouring Mill.

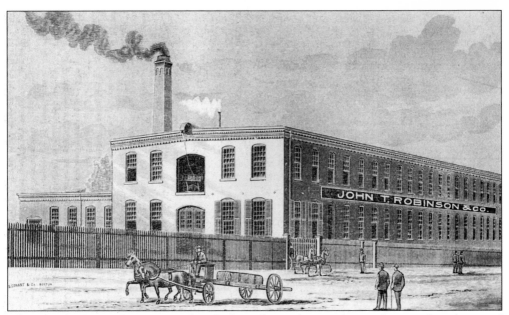

John T. Robinson & Company produced a line of paper box machinery for paper box shops and manufacturing purposes. Specialties of the company were power and foot cutters, round and oval cutters, rotary card cutters, rotary stripping machines, patent iron-frame shears, and Robinson's patent scorer.

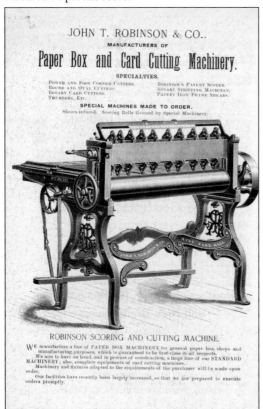

The Robinson Scoring and Cutting Machine was embossed "John T. Robinson & Co., Hyde Park, Mass." and was one of many special machines made to order.

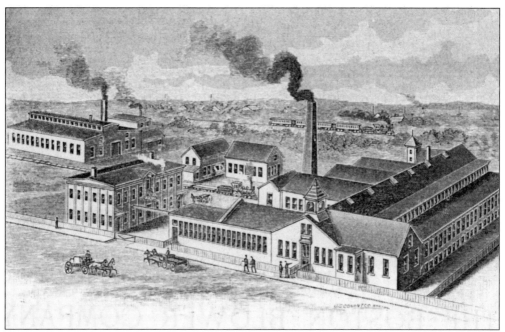

The Brainard Milling Machine Company manufactured milling machines, automatic gate-cutting machinery, mill grinding machinery, and the various tools and appliances used in operating these machines.

Amos H. Brainard was general superintendent, treasurer, and manager of the Brainard Milling Machine Company. After his move to Hyde Park in 1858, he served as a member of the board of selectmen and was the first president of the Hyde Park Historical Society.

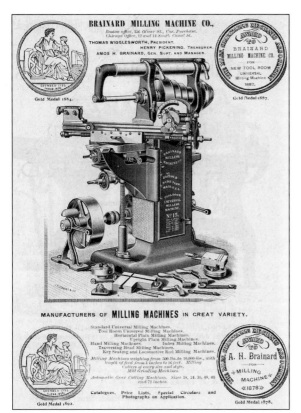

The milling machines produced by Brainard received gold medals from the Massachusetts Charitable Mechanic Association in 1878, 1884, 1887, and 1892 for their exceptionally high quality.

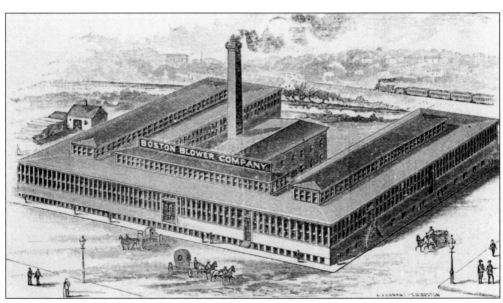

The Boston Blower Company was built in 1885 and manufactured heating and ventilation engines, paper bag machinery, envelope machinery, shoe machinery, air compressors, and ice machines.

Miss A.M. Lougee was the president of the Clifton Manufacturing Company, which produced rubber clothing. Miss Lougee was described as "the only woman in the rubber trade and one of the few successful business women of Boston."

John Sheehan was a shoe dealer in Hyde Park at the turn of the century.

Tileston & Hollingsworth was founded by Edmund Pitt Tileston and Mark Hollingsworth in 1805. Paper has been produced along the Neponset River since 1728, when John Boies and Hugh McLean, as Boies & McLean, began the production of rag paper in Milton. Used for legal documents, wills, testaments, and currency, paper was an important part of the area's economy.

The B.F. Sturtevant Company was founded in 1863 by Benjamin Franklin Sturtevant. In 1901, the plant in Hyde Park was opened, producing heating and ventilating equipment, unit heaters, ventilating fans, coal-burning blowers, drying equipment, vacuum-cleaning equipment, and many other products.

Thomas Leyland and Company, Inc. was a Readville factory that produced gums, dextrines, soluble starches, soluble oils, softeners, and bleachers blue. The factory was conveniently located adjacent to the railroad.

The Bay State Upholstery Company was founded in 1926 on Business Street. Upholstering everything from sofas and chairs to hassocks and stools, the company had upwards of two hundred employees at the height of its business.

John Bleakie was a native of Harwick, Roxburghshire, Scotland, and was considered "the pioneer in the weaving of fancy woolens in this country." His Hyde Park Woolen Mills developed into a prominent manufacturer of woolen goods; it continued operating for years under the direction of Bleakie's sons.

John S. Bleakie, the son of John Bleakie, maintained the extensive manufacturing business his father established in Hyde Park. Prominent in the wool trade, he was recognized as "a master in his profession."

The shop of Henry A. Rich provided paper hanging, graining, painting, and glazing at "Boston Prices" for the residents of Hyde Park. In addition to the provision of these services, Rich also stocked staple goods such as flour and grain to augment his business.

The F.W. Darling Company provided hay for livestock in the late nineteenth century. Here, employees pose with a horse-drawn hay wagon leaving the barn for local deliveries.

The Hyde Park Water Tower stored drinking water for town residents during drought season. The wood-shingled tower on the right encased a spiral staircase that connected the cupola to the tower by means of an exterior ramp.

PUMPING STATION, HYDE PARK, MASS.

The pumping station of the Hyde Park Water Company began the task of refining sewerage in the late nineteenth century. In 1888 the company had "22.35 miles of mains, the number of water takers at the present time being 1,005."

Eleven
Scenic Hyde Park

The estate of Henry Sturgis Grew was an extensive tract of land that was partly in Hyde Park, Roslindale, and West Roxbury. Known as "Grew's Woods," the area is perpetuated in the Stony Brook Reservation and the George Wright Golf Course. In the foreground, the Stony Brook passes a bucolic section of the estate at the turn of the century.

The Neponset River has a sense of serenity, as seen in this photograph taken in 1895 below the Fairmount Avenue bridge.

This landscape of a pasture in Hyde Park was painted by John J. Enneking. With grazing sheep and clouds passing overhead, this scene was characteristic of the rural charms of Hyde Park in the nineteenth century.

John J. Enneking was one of the most important of the impressionistic painters in America. Born in Minster, Auglaize County, Ohio, he moved to Hyde Park when he married Miss Mary Eliot, a local girl.

The painting *Stone Bridge at Fairmount* was one of Enneking's series of scenes along the Neponset River. With its muted tones and bold brush strokes, Enneking's impressionistic art was to be widely acclaimed during his lifetime.

In this photograph of October 1890, the Neponset River flows through Hyde Park. With an abundance of greenery, rock formations, and natural charm, Hyde Park in the nineteenth century was a place of beauty less than 7 miles from Boston.

Looking west from Sally's Rock, this area of Hyde Park in 1895 was, remarkably, a relatively undeveloped section of the town.

Looking south from Sally's Rock, a new neighborhood has been created in the area of Metropolitan Avenue near the Greenwood School (shown here on the right). In the last two decades of the nineteenth century, houses sprang up as if by magic in the newly incorporated town.

West Street in Hyde Park runs from Poplar Street to Railroad Avenue. The trees that shaded this country road near the George Wright Golf Course are shown here at the turn of the century.

Grew's Woods was originally bisected by West Street. On either side of this street are mature trees that give a sense of the countryside just outside the big city.

These friends bicycled to Grew's Woods at the turn of the century. While their companions lounge on the ground, the ladies pose with a Columbia bicycle.

The water pump at the entrance of Grew's Woods offered a refreshing drink of cool spring water. A path, on the right, leads into the woods for those "communing" with nature.

TURTLE POND & SUMMER HOUSE, HYDE PARK, MASS.

A summer house was built on the bank of Turtle Pond in the Stony Brook Reservation. Set amidst trees that shaded it and kept it cool during the summer, this dwelling must have provided a pleasant place to rest and to contemplate nature.

John Gately was known as the "Hermit of Grew's Woods." An Englishman by birth, Gately came to this country in 1847, laying claim to a small section of Henry Sturgis Grew's estate. He later built this hut, where he died in 1875.

The interior of Gately's hut was filled with birds, rabbits, snakes, and frogs that he stuffed and later sold to support his meager existence. He built bird cages during the winter, which he would sell in the spring.

Twelve

The Civil War
and the GAR

The Grand Army of the Republic marches up Fairmount Avenue on Memorial Day in 1905. The GAR symbolized fraternity, charity, and loyalty; the Timothy Ingraham Post # 121 in Hyde Park was organized in 1870 and named for Colonel and Brevet Brigadier General Timothy Ingraham of the 18th and 38th Massachusetts Volunteers. A band preceded the marching veterans, and a group of enthusiastic neighborhood boys trailed behind them.

The wood barracks at Camp Meigs survived for three decades following the Civil War. By 1890, as the Readville Trotting Park was being laid out, these barracks were moved and adapted as homes in Readville.

The Farrington Cannoneers had trials in Grew's Woods on July 4, 1890, in Hyde Park. Young men, as well as veterans of the Civil War, are shown here performing their maneuvers as a group of interested spectators looks on.

The Fife and Drum Corps of
Camp #146, Sons of Veterans,
poses on the steps of the Hyde
Park Library on Memorial Day
1905. In their dapper uniforms,
they were a popular group a
century ago.

Three residents of Hyde Park
pose in their uniforms in 1904
during the National
Encampment of the Grand Army
of the Republic in Boston. From
left to right are: Frank E. Conley
(a veteran of the Spanish
American War), Robert
McKeown (a veteran of the
Civil War), and Albert C. Clapp
(a veteran of the Mexican War).

Acknowledgments

I would like to thank the officers and the curators of the Hyde Park Historical Society for the use of the majority of the photographs used in this book. The collection is housed in Weld Hall at the Hyde Park Branch, Boston Public Library. My sincere thanks to Nancy Hannon, president of the Hyde Park Historical Society; George Merry, vice president; Ethel Reed, recording secretary; Alfred Harcourt, treasurer; and curators John Antoniazzi, Nicholas Costa, Robert Hannan, Ruth Highbee, Claire Pauley, Mary Pitts, Mary Stanton, and George Tarallo.

I would also like to thank the following for their interest and continued support: Daniel J. Ahlin, Anthony and Lorna Palumbo Bognanno, Paul and Helen Graham Buchanan, Edward W. Gordon, James Z. Kyprianos, Alice Imbaro Palumbo, Reverend Michael J. Parise, Dennis Ryan, Anthony and Mary Mitchell Sammarco, Rosemary Sammarco, William Varrell, and Barbara Wicker (branch librarian of the Hyde Park Branch, Boston Public Library).